D0131133

FBI AGENTS

BY ABBY COLICH

CAPSTONE PRESS

a capstone imprint

Blazers Books are published by Capstone Press,
1710 Roe Crest Drive, North Mankato, Minnesota 56003
www.mycapstone.com

Copyright © 2018 by Capstone Press, a Capstone imprint. All rights reserved.
No part of this publication may be reproduced in whole or in part, or stored
in a retrieval system, or transmitted in any form or by any means, electronic,
mechanical, photocopying, recording, or otherwise, without written permission
of the publisher.

Library of Congress Cataloging-in-Publication Data
Names: Colich, Abby, author.
Title: FBI agents / by Abby Colich.
Description: North Mankato, Minnesota : Capstone Press, [2018] |
Series: Blazers. U.S. federal agents | Includes bibliographical references
    and index.
Identifiers: LCCN 2017039234 (print) | LCCN 2017047996 (ebook) |
    ISBN 9781543501452 (eBook PDF) | ISBN 9781543501414 (hardcover)
Subjects: LCSH: United States. Federal Bureau of Investigation—Juvenile
    literature. | Law enforcement—Juvenile literature.
Classification: LCC HV8144.F43 (ebook) | LCC HV8144.F43 C645 2018 (print) |
    DDC 363.250973—dc23
LC record available at https://lccn.loc.gov/2017039234

Editorial Credits
Nikki Bruno Clapper, editor; Kyle Grenz, designer; Svetlana Zhurkin, media
researcher; Katy LaVigne, production specialist

Photo Credits
Courtesy of the Federal Bureau of Investigations, 8–9, 13, 16, 17, 21, 22–23, 24,
25; Dreamstime: Brian Scantlebury, 11; iStockphoto: Bliznetsov, 29, g-stockstudio,
cover (front); Newscom: Sipa USA/Charlie Varley, 5, TNS/Wichita Eagle/
Bo Rader, 14, Zuma Press/Chris Thelen, 18, Zuma Press/David Becker, 6;
Shutterstock: B Brown, 19; U.S. Navy: Mass Communication Specialist 2nd Class
Justan Williams, 27

Design Elements by Shutterstock

Printed and bound in the USA.
010757S18

Table of
Contents

The FBI

You visit a crime scene. You take part in a **raid**. Then you help make an arrest. All of that happens in just one day. You are an FBI agent. You help **enforce** the laws of the United States.

---

raid—a sudden, surprise attack on a place; the FBI raids places to gather evidence

enforce—to make sure something happens

FBI stands for **Federal** Bureau of Investigation. The FBI works to stop and solve federal crimes. Sometimes local and state police need help. They call the FBI.

An FBI agent studies a crime scene.

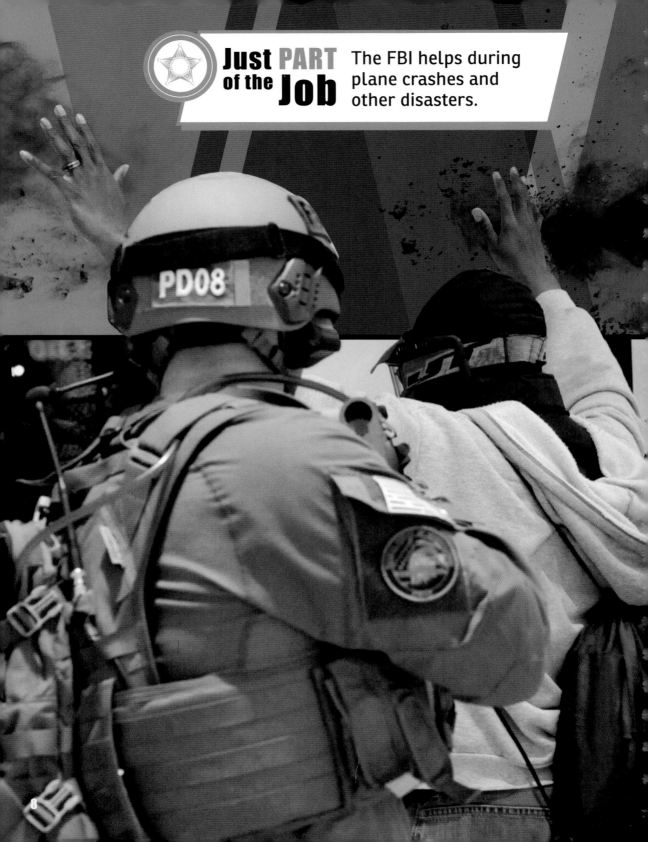

The FBI works on all kinds of crimes. Its top job is to stop **terrorism**. FBI agents solve child kidnappings too. They find bank robbers. They work to stop computer crimes.

terrorism—the use of violence and threats to frighten people

Just PART of the Job

The FBI has offices in other countries. They are called legal attachés or legats.

The FBI's head office is in Washington, D.C. It has other offices all over the country. The FBI may be needed at any time or at any place. It is always ready.

the FBI's head office

Working as an Agent

FBI agents do all kinds of jobs. They solve crimes. They find criminals and make arrests. They help during dangerous situations such as **standoffs**.

Just PART of the Job There are many other jobs at the FBI too. Some people are scientists. Others work in labs or with computers.

standoff—when a person or group prevents officials from acting, usually by threatening violence

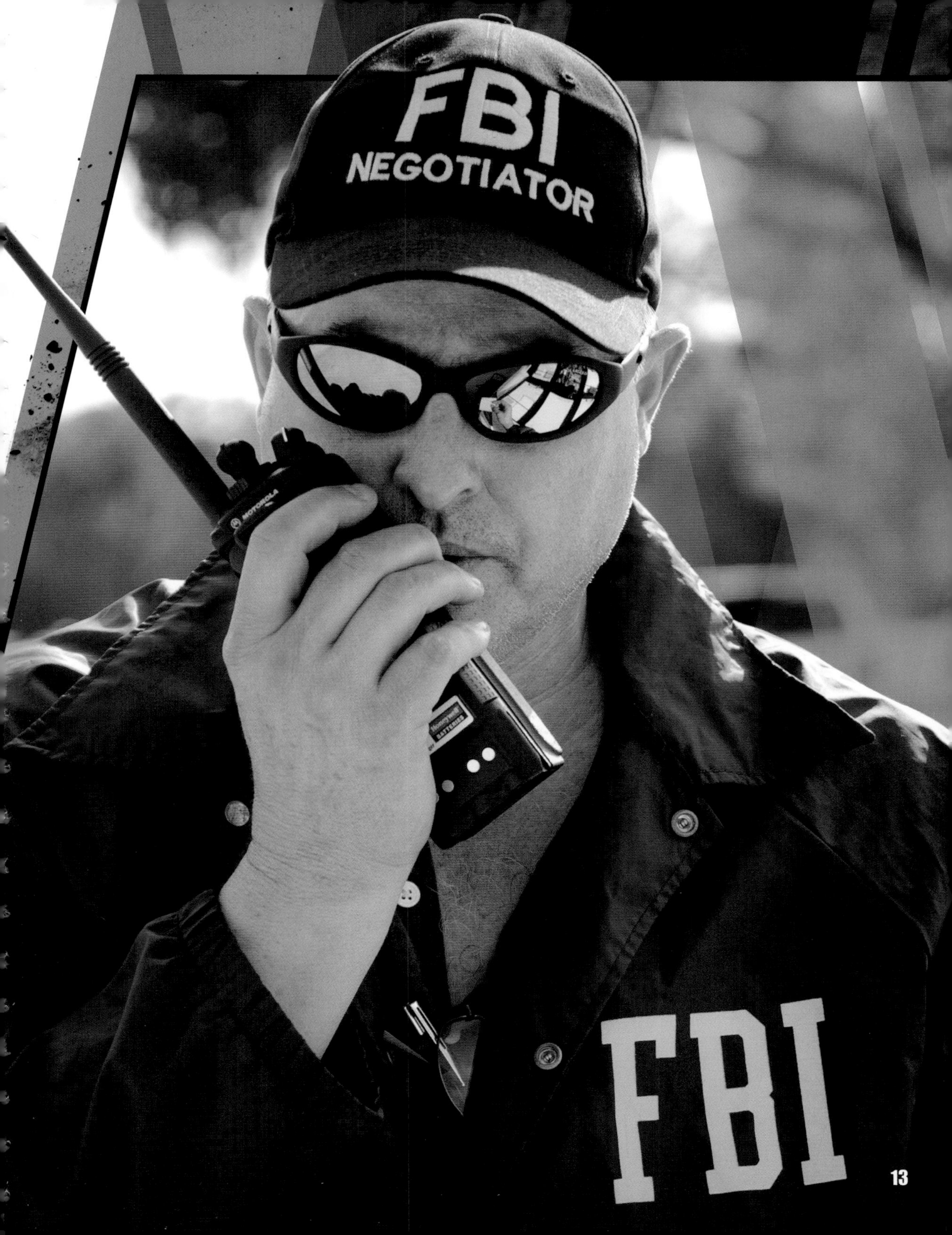
FBI
NEGOTIATOR
FBI

FBI agents work with U.S. **attorneys**. Together they look at **evidence**. They decide when to charge someone with a crime. Agents may **testify** in court about cases they worked on.

An FBI agent talks about his work with a U.S. attorney.

attorney—a person who is trained to advise people about the law

evidence—information, items, and facts that help prove something to be true or false

testify—to state facts in court during a trial

Getting a job with the FBI is not easy. Those who want a job must take a written test. Then they take a **polygraph**. They must pass a **background check**. FBI agents must be healthy.

a man taking a polygraph

polygraph—a device used to detect if a person is lying by tracking changes in body functions

background check—the process of looking up and compiling information about a person

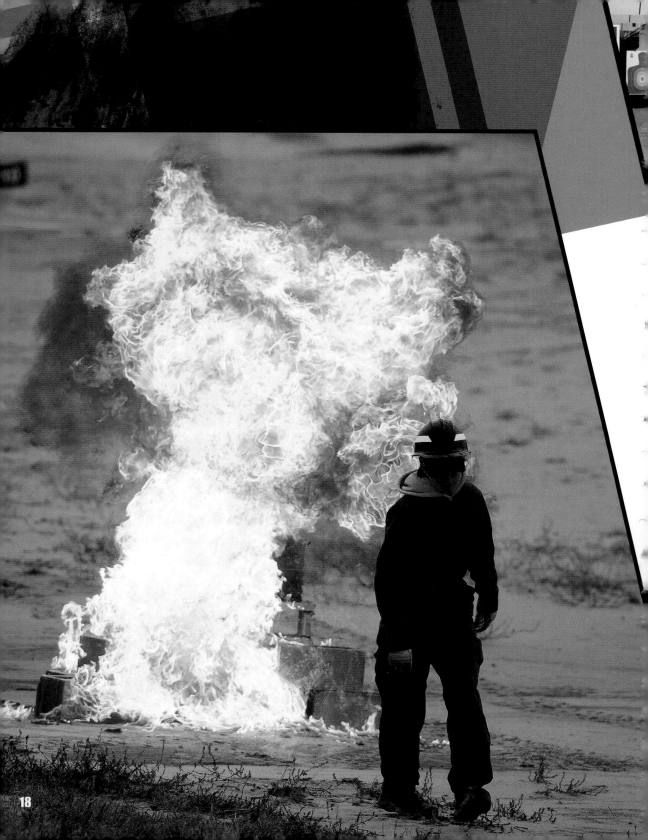

FBI agents train for up to 21 weeks. They learn about laws and crime. They go through tough physical training. They learn how to use weapons. They practice making arrests.

Just PART of the Job

Not everyone passes FBI training the first time. Some people have to start over from the beginning.

An FBI trainee learns how to use an explosive weapon.

Special Jobs

Some agents do just one type of work. They learn to do one thing very well. Some study how criminals act. Others fly helicopters. Some work on the **HAZMAT** team.

an FBI agent in a HAZMAT suit

HAZMAT—materials or items that are dangerous to life, property, or the environment; HAZMAT is short for hazardous material

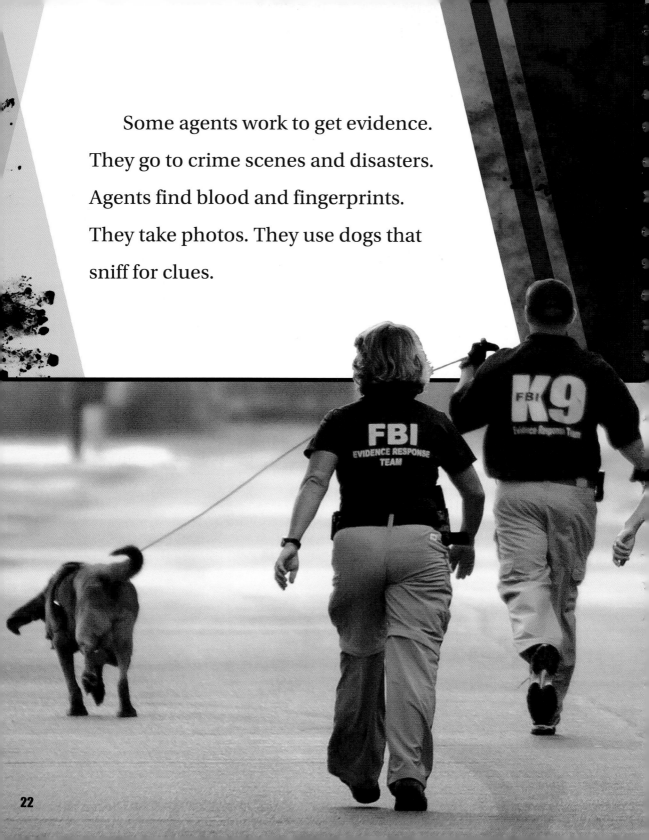

Some agents work to get evidence. They go to crime scenes and disasters. Agents find blood and fingerprints. They take photos. They use dogs that sniff for clues.

Just PART of the Job

Some FBI agents know how to find evidence underwater.

Just PART of the Job

A suit keeps bomb techs safe. The suit weighs 90 pounds (40.8 kilograms).

A package is left behind. Is it a bomb? FBI "bomb techs" will find out. These agents look for explosives. Robots help them check for danger.

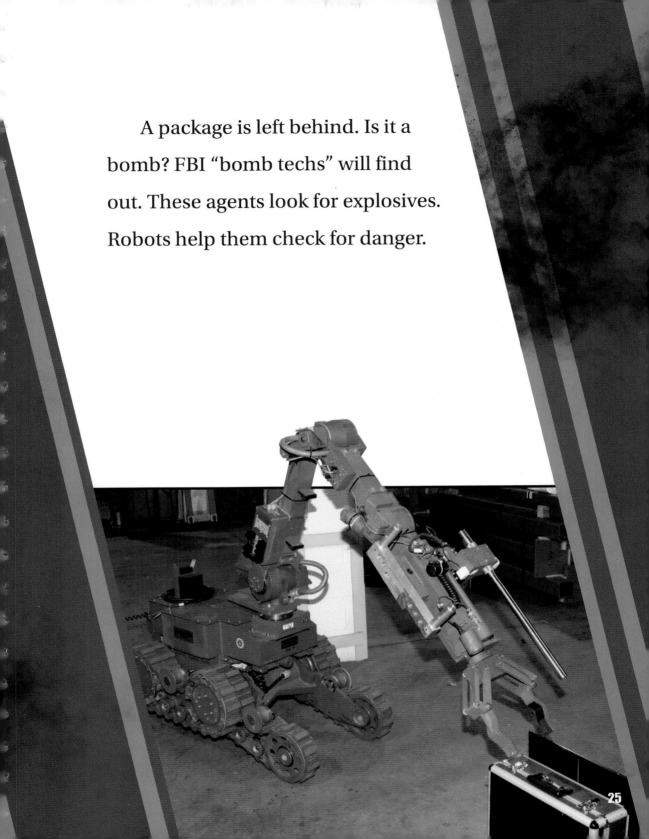

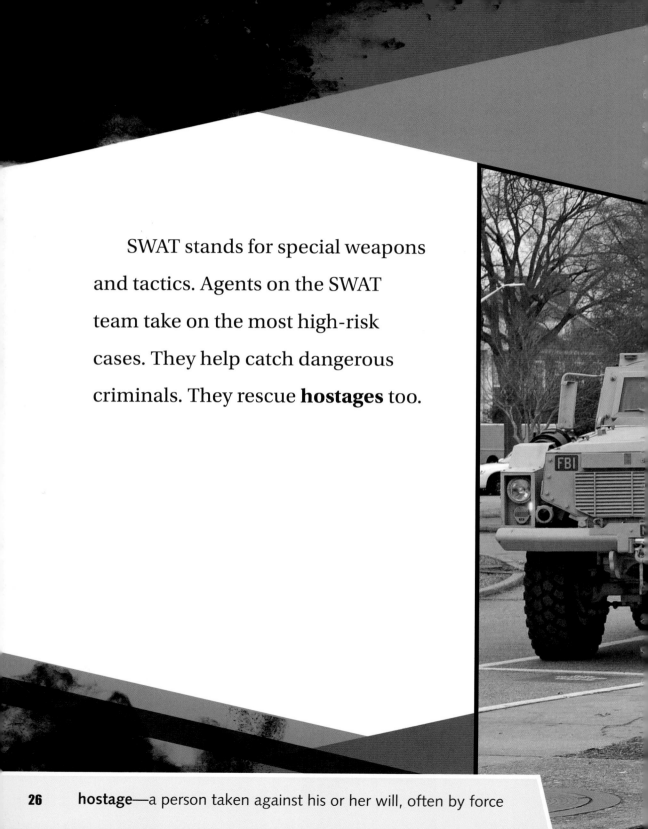

SWAT stands for special weapons and tactics. Agents on the SWAT team take on the most high-risk cases. They help catch dangerous criminals. They rescue **hostages** too.

hostage—a person taken against his or her will, often by force

Just PART of the Job

Special helmets, boots, kneepads, and gloves help keep the SWAT team safe. Sometimes agents wear gas masks.

Some agents work **undercover**. They are not allowed to say they work for the FBI. They use fake names. They pretend to be criminals. Then they catch the real criminals.

Just PART of the Job Some FBI agents go undercover for years at a time. They work hard to win people's trust.

undercover—done in secret, especially in spying activities

Glossary

attorney (uh-TUHR-nee)—a person who is trained to advise people about the law

background check (BAK-graund CHEK)—the process of looking up and compiling information about a person

enforce (in-FORS)—to make sure something happens

evidence (EV-uh-duhnss)—information, items, and facts that help prove something to be true or false

federal (FE-duh-ruhl)—having to do with the national government

HAZMAT (HAZ-mat)—materials or items that are dangerous to life, property, or the environment; HAZMAT is short for hazardous material

hostage (HOSS-tij)—a person taken against his or her will, often by force

polygraph (PAWL-ee-graf)—a device used to detect if a person is lying by tracking changes in body functions

raid (RAYD)—a sudden, surprise attack on a place; the FBI raids places to gather evidence

standoff (STAND-awf)—when a person or group prevents officials from acting, usually by threatening violence

terrorism (TER-urh-i-zuhm)—the use of violence and threats to frighten people

testify (TESS-tuh-fye)—to state facts in court during a trial

undercover (uhn-dur-KUHV-ur)—done in secret, especially in spying activities

Read More

Fraust, Daniel R. *A Career as an FBI Special Agent.* Federal Forces: Careers as Federal Agents. New York: PowerKids, 2016.

Mara, Wil. *FBI Special Agent.* 21st Century Skills Library: Cool Steam Careers. Ann Arbor, Mich.: Cherry Lake, 2016.

Whiting, Jim. *FBI Hostage Rescue and SWAT Teams.* U.S. Special Forces. Mankato, Minn.: Creative Education, 2015.

Internet Sites

Use FactHound to find Internet sites related to this book.

Visit *www.facthound.com*

Just type in 9781543501414 and go.

Check out projects, games and lots more at **www.capstonekids.com**

Index